WHAT IS THIS BOOK?

Before you get going, you are probably curious about what you will be reading over the course of the next four weeks. In *Witness: A 21-Day Easter Devotional*, you will discover more about the four authors that wrote what we refer to as "the Gospels." These are the first four books in the New Testament that share the Gospel, which is the Good News that Jesus Christ came to Earth to die for our sins so that we could have salvation and freedom in His name. Four men named Matthew, Mark, Luke, and John all attempted, with the great help of the Holy Spirit, to write an account that captures who Jesus is. These four witnesses to the power of Jesus are the inspiration for this devotional.

Not only will you learn about who each of them were, but you will also learn more about why their unique perspectives have helped countless believers know Jesus over the last 2,000 years. Each of these early believers had an important message to share about who Jesus was to them, and why He is the One He claimed to be: The Son of God. By looking at the four different Witness accounts, you are going to have a greater understanding of why we are incredibly blessed to have multiple accounts of Jesus' life, death, and resurrection. Matthew, Mark, Luke, and John all give a glimpse of Jesus that is unique to their experience and faith.

This brings us to you. The goal of this book is not only to teach you some cool stuff about the Gospel writers. It is also to encourage you to look at your unique experience with Jesus, and think about how you would share the Gospel (or Good News) with others!

HOW TO USE WITNESS:

This is a 21-Day devotional. There are really two different options you can choose from when reading through it. The first option is to read a new devotional every day. If you are someone that can stick to a plan, then this option is perfectly fine for you. However, when designing this devotional, we actually intended for most people to go with option two. In option two, you will begin the devotional four weeks before Easter. Each week, you will have seven days to complete five devotionals.

Every five days, you will learn about one specific gospel writer, how they viewed Jesus, and learn about some things that make their account of Jesus unique. Not only does this help you engage more fully with each of the gospel writers, but it also gives you some 'buffer days'. Maybe you wake up on a Monday and feel like you need to roll back over and sleep for another ten hours. That's ok! Your journey with *Witness* is not meant to be a burden to you. It is meant to be encouraging and easy to access.

If you miss a day here or there, you can still catch up! Keep at it. We know you've got this.

WEEK 1: MATTHEW

DAY 1 — WHO WAS MATTHEW?

Have you ever been sent a message that was written for someone else? A lot of Gentile (or non-Jewish) Christians can be tempted to say "wrong number" when it comes to the Gospel of Matthew because the language, imagery, and stories all seem to be written to someone else. One of the things that sets Matthew apart from the other three gospels is that it was written specifically to a Jewish audience. That means that there are things mentioned that might seem strange or unimportant to us. But Jewish people at the time would have heard these old prophecies and phrases and followed the implications very easily. It's a bit like having an inside joke with your friends... most people wouldn't understand why you are laughing until you explain it to them. But if you are with people who know the joke, you don't have to slow down and explain anything.

There is a strong belief in the Christian church that Matthew was named Levi before Jesus called him to be a disciple. And interestingly, Matthew is also known to have been a tax collector prior to his calling to follow Jesus (Matthew 9:9). Tax collectors were hated among the Jewish community because they tended to make their wages by charging people more than what they actually owed to their government. This common practice among tax collectors made them incredibly unpopular. People tended not to trust tax collectors because they took advantage of others. Despite this, Jesus called Matthew to be one of His followers. And if that wasn't enough, He called him to tell all of the people that likely thought he was a no-good lying thief about the life-changing power of the Gospel. Pretty incredible, right?

Matthew's witness is an important one, because it not only shows us why Jesus is the fulfillment of the Old Testament, but it also gives us a glimpse of how gracious God is. Jesus came with glory as the Son of God, but also with the humility of humanity. Matthew filled his witness with imagery of Jesus as the Promised Messiah, who was there to usher in a new kind of Kingdom that had no need to tax its citizens. Instead, it is a Kingdom of grace that is ruled forever by a perfect King- Jesus Christ.

DAY 2 — *JESUS AS THE PROMISED MESSIAH*

'And all the people were amazed, and said, 'Can this be the Son of David?' -Matthew 12:23

Each of the four Gospel authors viewed Jesus in a certain way, and they presented Him to their readers from that perspective. Matthew presented Jesus as the Promised Messiah. The word 'messiah' also means 'anointed.' Think about a King that is sworn into office- that is the imagery that surrounds the word messiah. With that in mind, Matthew wanted his readers to know that Jesus fulfilled the promises of the Old Testament and is the promised King. Matthew often makes references to these prophecies by using messiah-type titles that people give Jesus. For example, in the verse above, the people asked, "Can this be the Son of David?" which is a direct reference to 1 Samuel, where God's people are promised that a son of King David would one day establish an everlasting Kingdom.

Matthew wanted the people of God to understand that even though Jesus is the Messiah, or promised King, He was meant to be a King of an eternal Kingdom, not an earthly one.

Read Matthew 21:1-11.

As Jesus enters Jerusalem riding on a young donkey, the crowds welcomed Him into the city by waving palm branches in the air, shouting, "Hosanna in the highest!"

It was a common misconception of the people in that day to believe the Messiah would come as a political leader. They were expecting a leader who would overthrow the Roman Empire and establish a new earthly kingdom. Their shouts of "Hosanna" meant "save now." Later, when they realized Jesus was not a political leader, many did not believe He was the Promised Messiah. Sadly, the crowds did not see Jesus for who He really was. They placed their personal desires on Him instead.

We can be tempted to do the same. It's easy for us to mold Jesus into who we want Him to be instead of who He actually is. Jesus is not a person we manufacture. As Matthew tells us, He is the Promised Messiah of the Old Testament! And thankfully, He came to be so much more than a political leader or great teacher.

QUESTIONS

1. How are you tempted to make Jesus into someone He is not?

2. The word messiah also means 'anointed', similar to how we think of a king taking their throne. What does it mean for us that Jesus is the anointed King over an everlasting Kingdom?

3. How does viewing Christ as the Promised Messiah change your perspective of Him?

DAY 3 — MATTHEW: THE MAN

The book of the genealogy of Jesus Christ, the son of David, the son of Abraham. -Matthew 1:1

Sometimes in Christian art, you might see the four Gospels represented by four different images: a man for Matthew, a lion for Mark, an ox for Luke, and an eagle for John. These images originally come from a vision Ezekiel had in the Old Testament (Ezekiel 1:10-12), and they help us remember the different sides of Jesus each Gospel is trying to focus on.

Matthew is represented by the image of a man with wings. Why? Not because Matthew was some kind of angel, but because in Matthew's Gospel, he really emphasizes the humanity of Jesus! He even starts with a genealogy of Jesus right at the very beginning (Matt. 1:1-17). A genealogy lists out someone's ancestors in order, and Matthew lists Jesus' human ancestors all the way back to Abraham.

Now, like lots of people, you might be tempted to just skip right over genealogies in the Bible. Who wants to read a long list of confusing names, right? But these genealogies are actually there to tell us something really important! Jesus' genealogy tells us that Jesus is a real human being. After all, right after Matthew gives Jesus' genealogy, he tells us the story of Jesus' very humble human birth (Matt. 1:18-25). But even more than that, he tells us that Jesus is the ultimate, perfect human!

Jesus' genealogy is full of ancestors who were seriously flawed and sinful, even the big names like David and Abraham. But unlike His ancestors, Jesus never sinned. And it's Jesus' sinless, human life that makes it possible for you to be set free from the power of sin in your own life. Matthew's Gospel reminds us that Jesus is human like you and me, and He knows what it's like to live a hard human life. But it also reminds us that, unlike you and me, Jesus defeated sin, making a way for us to find salvation in Him.

QUESTIONS

1. Why do you think Matthew wanted to emphasize Jesus' humanity?

2. How might it change your relationship with Jesus to remember that He can relate to you and your experiences as a human being?

3. Is it comforting to remember that Jesus entered into our world to live a human life? Why or how?

DAY 4 — THE GROUND-SHAKING CRUCIFIXION

"And behold, the curtain of the temple was torn in two, from top to bottom. And the earth shook, and the rocks were split. The tombs also were opened. And many bodies of the saints who had fallen asleep were raised, and coming out of the tombs after his resurrection they went into the holy city and appeared to many." Matthew 27:51-53

So many movies have been made with the idea of life beyond death. Tombs breaking open sounds like something from a zombie movie – the dead coming to life. But tombs breaking open is exactly what happened after Jesus' ground-shaking crucifixion and resurrection. Take a moment to let that sink in... especially if you've never heard of this story. Now, read Matthew 27:51-53 and let's explore it together.

The Resurrection of Jesus is not only central to Easter, it's the center of the Christian faith. Believing Jesus died to pay the penalty for our sins and came back to life is the only way we can be saved. Without the resurrection, we are just people trying to do enough good for a reward we will never earn. We can never be perfect, and we can never be good enough. But because Jesus died and rose again, we are offered the chance to be saved!

Can you imagine what it would've been like to be in Jerusalem that day and actually see the bodies of dead people come to life? To witness a literal display of Jesus' power over death? Maybe you would see someone you knew, whose funeral you attended, just walking around talking about Jesus' victory over death. I don't know about you, but that would not only catch my attention – it'd create a core memory – something to never forget!

The thing is, those who believe in Jesus today are like those who came back to life from the tombs of the holy city. It may not feel as dramatic, but going from death to life is always a miracle. Just like those people in the tombs, you have been promised that even if you pass away, you will be raised again into eternity with Jesus Christ. And that is news worth spreading this Easter!

QUESTIONS

1. Imagine for a minute you saw people come back to life and walk around talking about Jesus. How do you think you would feel, think, and act?

2. How would you describe the significance of Jesus' ground-shaking crucifixion and resurrection to a friend?

3. Who are some people in your life who need to hear about the good news of Jesus? Write some names down and pray for these people to come to know Jesus. Pray and ask God to give you courage and the opportunity to share about Him with those people.

DAY 5 — PALM SUNDAY

"This took place to fulfill what was spoken by the prophet, saying, "Say to the daughter of Zion, 'Behold, your king is coming to you, humble, and mounted on a donkey, on a colt, the foal of a beast of burden.'" -Matthew 21:4-5

Have you ever had to wait a long time for something? Think about the end of a long school year. You've studied and worked hard for months, and finally, the promised summer vacation is right around the corner! Those final minutes on that last day of school can make pretty much anyone to want to jump out of their chair. After all of that waiting, summer vacation hits and you feel the intense joy of the freedom you had been waiting for!

One day, in the city of Jerusalem, the people of Israel celebrated the end of their waiting, because, at last, they saw the arrival of a King, riding on the back of a donkey. Kind of a weird sight to imagine right? The people of Israel are shouting "Hosanna!" And "Hallelujah!" to Jesus and all He's doing is riding a donkey into town.

Well, take a closer look at the verses above.

You see, Matthew is quoting the prophet Zechariah (Zechariah 9:9), which was written hundreds of years before the day Jesus arrived. Remember, Matthew was writing from the perspective of someone deep in Jewish culture, who would have known the implications of seeing a guy on a donkey entering Jerusalem. The people of Israel had been waiting on this day for centuries, and at long last here was Jesus doing exactly what the prophet said! Imagine seeing a 400-year-old promise fulfilled right before your eyes.

This day is often called Palm Sunday on the Christian calendar because the palm branch was not only used by the welcoming crowd to celebrate Jesus' arrival, but it was also a symbol of 'victory.' How awesome is that? Even before His death, Jesus is celebrated as having victory!

QUESTIONS

1. Why is it so important for Jesus to ride in on a donkey? Could He have chosen another way to enter?

2. How often do you celebrate Jesus' entrance into your own life? What might you do to celebrate Him more?

3. What promises of God do you see being fulfilled in your life right now?

WEEK 2: MARK

DAY 6 — WHO WAS MARK?

Mark is the shortest of the four Gospels, and some believe it may have been the first to be written. Although most of the stories in Mark can be found in Matthew and Luke, there is still a unique witness to who Jesus is and why it matters. Just like some of the other Gospel writers, the writer of Mark was not simply named 'Mark.' Instead, he holds the name John Mark, which can be shortened to either John or Mark.

What little we know about Mark is found in the Book of Acts, which is the "origin story" of the Christian church. Mark was not one of Jesus' twelve disciples. However, it appears from his witness that he was present within a regular group of people who followed Jesus around. What is more evident is that Mark was busy doing ministry during the days of the early Church. There are several references to Mark's location and work with the early church, both in the Book of Acts and Paul's letters to the different churches (Colossians, 2 Timothy, and 1 Peter). What we know is this: Mark seemed to have had a habit of running away from difficulty. In Acts, Barnabas and Paul even argue over an incident where Mark ran away (Acts 13). It appears that Barnabas may have had a little more patience for Mark because he was his cousin.

Mark's shortcomings were not too big for God to use him, though. And just like Mark, each of us has left opportunities to serve God on the table. The fact that Mark is now one of our four gospel writers is testimony enough to God's patience and perseverance with His people! Despite his Gospel being brief, it is still full of his admiration for Jesus. He shows us that Jesus is incredibly strong, and even though many people measure His strength by human standards, Mark challenges us to see an even greater Savior that can humbly take the throne and give grace beyond our understanding. This humble mercy is the real strength of Jesus Christ!

DAY 7 — JESUS AS THE SUFFERING SERVANT

"And he began to teach them that the Son of Man must suffer many things and be rejected by the elders and the chief priests and the scribes and be killed, and after three days rise again." -Matthew 8:31

Each of the Gospel writers displays a different side of Jesus. Remember that Matthew presented Jesus as the "Promised Messiah." But Mark presents Jesus as the "Suffering Servant." Why? Because Mark wants his readers to know that Jesus' purpose was to suffer and die as payment, or atonement for our sins.

Read Mark 8:31-33.

In the verses before these, Peter confesses Jesus as the Messiah. From there, Jesus tells the disciples that the role of the Messiah is to suffer. He will be rejected by many and will be killed. Peter is blown away by this. He did not like what Jesus was saying. How could the mighty Messiah come to Earth to suffer?

Although Peter did not understand the will of God, Jesus did. He came to seek and save the lost. He came to provide salvation for the world. That would mean suffering, sacrifice, and rejection. It would mean the Cross. All of the necessary sacrificial steps that are foreshadowed in the Old Testament would have remained unfulfilled if Jesus had not done these things. If Peter had taken a step back, he would see that through suffering, Jesus was bringing the greatest gift imaginable. Through suffering, there would be everlasting life for God's people.

At times, we feel there is no purpose in our suffering, and we believe we have a better plan than God. Sometimes, we might even criticize God as Peter did. However, we must hold onto the image that Mark gives us.

Suffering doesn't stop God's plans- it does not have that kind of power. Even in the worst of circumstances, God is working. Nothing is out of His plans. Whatever you are walking through and whatever you will walk through, know that He is the Suffering Servant, and your pain will not be wasted. God is able to take evil and turn it into good.

QUESTIONS

1. When you think of Jesus suffering for the sake of His people, how does that impact your view of Him?

2. How have you seen suffering being used by God to accomplish something greater?

3. Even though Peter challenged Jesus in the passage above, Jesus still used Peter to build the Church. What does that tell you about God's character?

DAY 8 — *MARK: THE LION*

"The beginning of the gospel of Jesus Christ, the Son of God."- Mark 1:1

Mark is represented by the image of a lion. Why might this be? When you think of lions, what do you think of? If the movie, The Lion King, comes to mind, you're actually not far off! Long before that movie came out, lions represented royalty. The image of the royal lion is fitting for the Gospel of Mark, because Mark tells us in the very first line that he's writing about the King: "Jesus Christ, the Son of God" (Mark 1:1).

In case you weren't sure, "Christ" isn't Jesus' last name. It is a special title that means "Anointed King." Mark emphasizes throughout his Gospel that he is writing about Jesus the King, the Lord of all. (Remember, Matthew also emphasized this, but used the word 'Messiah' most of the time to get his point across). But Jesus isn't some king who sits off in His palace far away from His people and safe from any danger. Like a lion, Jesus is a king who entered into the wilderness of this sinful world and put Himself on the Cross for you and me.

Mark quotes the Old Testament prophet Isaiah at the beginning of his Gospel: *"Behold, I send my messenger before your face, who will prepare your way, the voice of one crying in the wilderness: Prepare the way of the Lord, make his paths straight"* (Mark 1:2-3). It turns out that hundreds of years before Jesus was born to Mary, the prophet Isaiah was given a 'sneak peek' if you will, of what was to come. His prophecies were fulfilled not only in some of the details of Jesus' arrival, but also in the arrival of John the Baptist. John the Baptist was this messenger who cried out in the wilderness to anyone who would listen that Jesus, the King, was coming and that He would bring salvation with Him.

Mark's Gospel bears witness to the fact that Jesus did come. He entered the wilderness and blazed through it like a royal lion on a mission to save His kingdom. And that salvation extends even to today, to you and me!

QUESTIONS

1. The image of Jesus as a lion in the wilderness reminds us that this sinful world is often a wild, scary place. How have you experienced this?

2. What "wilderness" might you be going through right now that you need Jesus to save you from or comfort you through?

3. Why do you think Mark wanted to emphasize that Jesus is King and Lord? What is Jesus the King and Lord of, and why does that matter to us today?

DAY 9

"And a young man followed him, with nothing but a linen cloth about his body. And they seized him, but he left the linen cloth and ran away naked." -Mark 14:51-52

Each gospel has it's own unique stories about Jesus' time on Earth. Mark is no different. In today's devotional, you are going to be looking at a somewhat funny story that shows us how strange the events surrounding that first Easter really were.

Think about this question: What are some things that scare you: spiders, snakes, heights? We all have things we are afraid of. Imagine being so scared of something that you literally run right out of your clothes to get away from it. Sounds like a scene from a cartoon, am I right? Well, that is exactly what happened to one of Jesus' followers when Jesus was arrested. Check out Mark 14:51-52.

There are several beliefs about why this is included here, but not in the other gospels. A very common thought in the Church is that it was Mark himself who ran straight out of his clothes. If it was Mark, he could've easily left this unflattering part out. But much respect for Mark if he is willing to share so honestly about his fear. Sitting wherever you are now, it can be easy to judge the early believers for scattering in fear. What do we do when persecution, or sometimes just the threat of being made fun of or thought of as weird because of our faith, arises? Do we run from the situation, or see it as a chance to stand with Jesus?

Jesus told us persecution would be the price of following Him. God also tells us not to fear because He is with us (Joshua 1:9). But standing in the face of fear is easier said than done. When we remind ourselves that God is with us, and He is stronger and mightier than any obstacle or danger we face, it gives us courage. It also gives us a heavenly perspective of what is going on around us. Next time you face something scary, remember the God who created the Universe and who conquered death is on your side.

QUESTIONS

1. How is your reputation directly impacted by your relationship with Jesus?

2. Many people believe that Mark is talking about himself in today's passage. What does it teach us about God's character, that even though Mark ran away from Jesus in a time of distress, God still used him to share a witness about who Jesus is?

3. If you had been the one to run straight out of your clothes when you saw that Jesus was being arrested, would you have included that detail in your witness? Why or why not?

DAY 10 — *THE LAST SUPPER*

"And he said to them, 'This is my blood of the covenant, which is poured out for many.'"
-Mark 14:24

In the book of Genesis, chapter 15, God meets with Abraham to seal a covenant promise with him to bless his family line. In those days, an agreement this big was sealed with the blood of sacrificial animals to symbolize to those involved how serious the covenant was. If you still aren't sure what the word covenant means, that's okay! There are a lot of elements involved with biblical covenants, but they all essentially serve the same purpose: To define the relationship between two parties and set expectations for the relationship moving forward.

In Mark 14, Jesus sits down for a meal with the friends that had been traveling with Him, mainly His twelve disciples. This was not just any meal, this was the Passover feast, a time when the people of Israel remembered that God spared them from death in Egypt thanks to the blood of a sacrificial lamb. In the middle of the meal, Jesus took some bread and wine and passed it around to the disciples. He then said that the bread represented His body and the wine represented His blood. This may seem odd to you at first, but if you look at Jesus' words, it's clear what He was showing His friends.

Jesus is referencing His own death, and talking about why it has to happen. Just like in the agreement with Abraham so long ago, Jesus knew that if He wanted to form a covenant this large and powerful with His people, His own blood had to be part of it. Depending on your church, you likely honor this moment by participating in a similar practice multiple times a year. Not only is this moment one of the last moments of calm before the arrest of Jesus, but it is also His most direct indication that He would lay down His life for the sake of ours. This was indeed a Last Supper, but it was also the Lord's Supper!

QUESTIONS

1. How might the disciples have felt when Jesus passed out the bread and wine?

2. Why is it important for the Church to remember "The Lord's Supper?"

3. What would you tell someone if they asked you about what the Lord's Supper represents?

WEEK 3: LUKE

DAY 11 — WHO WAS LUKE?

It is easy to look at Luke and say that he was a Gentile (non-Jewish person) physician, and then move on. But Luke is perhaps the most interesting of the four Gospel writers! Do you know that kid that is always taking very detailed notes in class? Or even the kid that can rattle off endless facts about a certain sports team, video game, or book series? Luke is a little bit like that. He was obsessed with all the details, and for our benefit, he not only wrote a detail-rich version of the Gospel, but he also authored the book of Acts, which tells us all about the early church. If you take the time to read his witness, you will see that it is full of so many stories from all kinds of perspectives. This is because Luke was not an eyewitness himself. He interviewed others and collected stories about who Jesus was and how He impacted the lives of those around Him. In fact, most of Luke's writing suggests that he came to faith during one of the Pauline missions!

As a Gentile, Luke did not have a background in Jewish studies, but he was able to write a Gospel from the perspective of a non-Jewish person. This witness has been hugely important for the Church because an overwhelming amount of believers in the world have a similar background. In fact, many of you reading this devotional would fit into the non-Jewish category! His curiosity and writing skills were part of the reason that he eventually joined Paul in some of his later missions. Luke went from being thought of as "an unclean Gentile" to being a very important part of the early Church's development.

While you read about some of the different stories and perspectives found in the gospel of Luke, keep in mind that most of these stories are meant to show that God's redemption is for ALL people. Whether you feel like you are worthy or not, Luke wants his witness to remind you that Jesus came to save the outcasts.

DAY 12 — JESUS AS THE SON OF MAN

"And Jesus said to him, 'Today salvation has come to this house, since he also is a son of Abraham. For the Son of Man came to seek and to save the lost.'" – Luke 19:9-10

In Luke's Gospel account, Jesus is presented as the Son of Man. Luke wants his readers to see that Jesus is fully man even though He is also fully God. Throughout this book, Jesus' humanity is emphasized.

Read Luke 19:2-10.

As Jesus is passing through Jericho, imagine the crowds lined up to get a glimpse of Him. There were probably a lot of people, which can make it hard to see. So being resourceful, a short man climbs a tree so he can get a better view of Jesus. This man, Zacchaeus, was a tax collector. Not only that, but he was a chief tax collector. You may recall from our earlier devotionals that tax collectors made their fortunes off of being deceitful. People hated tax collectors.

However, Jesus had a different attitude toward Zacchaeus. When He sees Zacchaeus in the tree, He tells him to come down so that He can stay at Zacchaeus' house. We read that Zacchaeus joyfully welcomed Jesus. Zacchaeus was very much changed by the encounter. Zacchaeus' encounter with Jesus shows us that Jesus has a heart for everyone. It doesn't matter what you look like, how much you have, what you've done, and what you've accomplished. Jesus has come to seek and save the lost.

Zacchaeus probably felt hated by many, alone in life, and unloved by God. Sometimes, we think we have out-sinned the grace of God. We can look at ourselves and think there is no possible hope for our salvation. But this is the gospel that Luke wants us to hear: Jesus is the Son of Man, just as He is the Son of God. He understands what it is to be human. He sees us for who we are regardless of who we are! Because of Jesus' humanity, He can relate to us. Jesus experienced everything you are walking through. Jesus understands the battles you are fighting, and He will not leave you to fight them alone, no matter how far away you feel. One of Luke's main goals in his Gospel is to show us that Jesus' humanity is one of the most wonderful things about Him.

QUESTIONS

1. How does knowing Jesus is able to sympathize with your weakness change the way you view temptation?

2. Luke emphasized the humanity of Jesus. What are some reasons that he might have done this?

3. List some experiences that you have 'as a human'. After you've made your list, think about how Jesus might have experienced some of these things, or something similar. (For example, maybe you've been on a road trip with your family. Jesus also traveled many times with His family!)

DAY 13 — *LUKE: THE OX*

"Lord, now you are letting your servant depart in peace, according to your word; for my eyes have seen your salvation that you have prepared in the presence of all peoples, a light for revelation to the Gentiles, and for glory to your people Israel."-Luke 2:29-32

The third Gospel is often represented with the image of an ox (or a bull). If you're not sure what an ox is, that's okay. You may not have seen an ox in real life, but in biblical times an ox was a big farm animal that was used to pull and carry heavy things. Up until the time of Jesus, though, they were also used for something even more important: sacrifices.

In the Old Testament, God's people had to make animal sacrifices to receive forgiveness for their sins. This was something they had to do over and over again, and they often used animals like oxen for these sacrifices. So why is Luke represented with an ox? Because Jesus provided the ultimate sacrifice with His death on the Cross. This is what Luke wants to emphasize in his witness.

Luke even starts out his Gospel with a priest making a sacrifice at the temple! Zechariah, the priest, was in the temple when an angel came to him and told him that his wife, Elizabeth, would have a baby that would prepare everyone for the Lord (Luke 1:5-17). Remember that voice in the wilderness from Mark? Their baby was John the Baptist, who told everyone that Jesus was coming!

And when Jesus came, He made Himself the ultimate sacrifice so priests like Zechariah would never have to sacrifice an ox again. Unlike an ox, Jesus was the perfect sacrifice whose blood could cover the sins of the whole world once and for all. His death on the Cross earned forgiveness for all of your sins so that you can know God and have eternal life with Him. And Jesus made that sacrifice willingly because of His deep, deep love for you.

QUESTIONS

1. Can you imagine having to make an animal sacrifice every time you sinned? What do you think that was like for the people of God?

2. Think about this: How can Jesus be both a human and the Lord? How can He be both the Lord and a sacrifice for humankind?

3. If your witness of Jesus had an image to describe it- like the ox- what do you think it would be and why?

DAY 14 — FORGIVENESS FOR THE THIEF

"Then he said, 'Jesus, remember me when you come into your kingdom.' Jesus answered him, 'Truly I tell you, today you will be with me in paradise.'"- Luke 23:42-43

When you wake up each morning, what do you do? Maybe you brush your teeth, take a shower, etc. We get cleaned up and dressed up to head out into the world for the day....unless it's pajama day at your school, and you can just roll out of bed. Maybe because it's a daily habit to get cleaned up to head out into the world, we can sometimes feel the pressure to get cleaned up to get close to God. We feel the pressure to do everything right before we can go hang out with God.

Read Luke 23:32-43. As you do, notice the two criminals hanging next to Jesus. One guy mocks Jesus, but the other talks with Him, and shows Him respect. Let's talk about the one who was respectful to Jesus. This guy is guilty and hanging on a cross, so he can't clean himself up. There are no more opportunities for him to right his wrongs. He knows something that is important for us all to know: we are dependent on Jesus' forgiveness, and we really don't have anything to offer in exchange for that. Look at how Jesus responds to this no-good criminal: Jesus lovingly and graciously offers him not only forgiveness, but eternal life. Wow! Jesus sees through this man's brokenness and because of his faith in Jesus, he receives forgiveness. Those watching, including us, are witnesses to Jesus' forgiveness even in the middle of Jesus' greatest pain.

Today, let the forgiveness for the thief be a reminder to you of the forgiveness Jesus offers you. Boldly ask Jesus for forgiveness. Jesus can change your life story into one that is full of His love and light. Just like Jesus invited the criminal to be with Him forever, Jesus offers you the same amazing invitation. You can be forgiven and join Him in paradise. We can live in the freedom Jesus offers us and offer it to others! We can become better witnesses for Jesus when we remember the depth of His love, grace, and forgiveness for ourselves and for others.

QUESTIONS

1. What do you need to ask Jesus' forgiveness for? How can you ask Him for that forgiveness?

2. When you think of forgiving others, what do you think is hardest about doing that?

3. Who around you might need to hear for the first time, or as a reminder, of Jesus' amazing invitation to be forgiven and to be with Him?

DAY 15 — *CRUCIFIXION*

"And Jesus said, 'Father, forgive them, for they know not what they do.' And they cast lots to divide his garments." – Luke 23:34

Read Luke 23:26-38. How can it be that one of the most heartbreaking passages in the Bible is also one of the most important?

Take a moment and think about the life Jesus lived. He was a poor man who walked from town to town healing people, showing miracles, teaching about love, and proclaiming that God's peace had come for all people.

However, Jesus received punishment for crimes He didn't commit, but He faced an all-out rejection from the people involved in His trial. He was mocked and abused, and yet... Jesus responds with compassion. The people who took these horrifying "extra steps" to make His death even more painful were a part of one of His final pleas to God the Father.

His body was ripped apart by a whip and nailed to a cross. He felt the laughs and scorn of the people who He loved and saw many of His friends abandon Him. He experienced true suffering and what does He say to God? "Forgive them..."

Jesus is the only one who could have that kind of mercy. The crowds mocked Him for not destroying them in His suffering. However, instead of wrath, Jesus chose His own death because He knew that only by His death, would the people He loved find freedom from their sins.

Jesus embraced the humiliation and torment so that you would not have to. He took on the pain of rejection, and still sought to offer forgiveness!

QUESTIONS

1. Why would Jesus suffer willingly?

2. Imagine for a moment that you are present at the crucifixion of Jesus Christ. What feelings would you have about Jesus, and the others around you? How might you respond when Jesus asks the Father to forgive those who are being awful to Him?

3. In what ways can you honor the sacrifice of Jesus?

WEEK 4: JOHN

DAY 16 — WHO WAS JOHN?

Do you have a friend who is really into myths and legends? Perhaps they are a big reader, and they love telling you about the creatures in their favorite book. Or maybe you are the person telling everyone about a show you love that contains all sorts of mysterious characters and plot lines. This is essentially the style that John used to tell others about Jesus!

Unlike the other three witnesses, John embraced the divine mystery of Jesus and plunged into it with excitement. He wanted people to get caught up in how mythical all of it seemed, only to remind them that this was indeed real. Unlike the legends of the Greek and Roman gods of the day, Jesus genuinely walked and talked with His followers. Jesus was all of the divine, while also being in full human flesh. John points out the mystical, and he shows us that Jesus did not just suffer for our bodies, but also for our souls.

It is commonly believed that the John who wrote the Gospel of John is the same one who was called with his brother to be a disciple of Jesus (Mark 1:19-20). Based on what we can tell of him from the other Gospel accounts, John had a lot of zeal (or passion) about what he believed. This can occasionally be seen in how he tells different stories from Jesus' ministry. As you get to know the last of the four witnesses, think about how different your own witness might be. Just like John, it may seem different from some of your friends, but that is okay! John shows us that God has a place for all sorts of people in His kingdom.

DAY 17 — JESUS AS THE SON OF GOD

"And the Word became flesh and dwelt among us, and we have seen his glory, glory as of the only Son from the Father, full of grace and truth."- John 1:14

The Book of John presents Jesus as the Son of God. John shows us that Jesus is divine and 100 percent God in human flesh.

Read John 4:7-14. In this story, Jesus meets a Samaritan woman at the water well. This lady had come during the middle of the day to get her water so she wouldn't see anyone else. You may know what it's like to not want to be seen. But she finds Jesus there, and He has every intention of seeing her and speaking with her. He tells her if she drinks the water from the well, she'll get thirsty again; but, if she drinks the water He's offering, then she will never thirst again.

What is Jesus talking about? Jesus is promising life! Or, more specifically, the living water that represents eternal life. At the time, many women could only find their livelihood in marriage. The culture was set in such a way, that if a woman could not find a husband who had food, money, and shelter for her, she would do without. This woman clearly had a hard time finding and hanging on to these things. She seemed to be living the life of a stray cat- collecting what little scraps she could from multiple homes. This resulted in her having multiple husbands. Seeing her shame and despair, Jesus addresses her with the truth. Jesus tells her He's the only one who can bring life. Although she has sought life from multiple men and found herself unfulfilled, she was now being offered a big, beautiful, eternal life from a single source (Jesus, the Son of God).

Why is it important that John presents Jesus as the Son of God? Well, it means that Jesus can give life because He's the Creator of life. He can promise satisfaction because He designed satisfaction. He can fulfill because He is enough. Just like this woman, we try to quench our thirst in all kinds of ways...through relationships, grades, sports, possessions, and worldly pursuits. Yet, we will constantly find ourselves coming up empty. Only Jesus can satisfy. Only He can bring fulfillment!

QUESTIONS

1. How do you relate to the woman at the well?

2. What are ways you can remind yourself that only Jesus can satisfy your soul?

3. When we refer to Jesus as the Son of God and the Son of Man, what does that mean? How do you explain that both are true?

DAY 18 — JOHN: THE EAGLE

"For everyone who does wicked things hates the light and does not come to the light, lest his works should be exposed. But whoever does what is true comes to the light, so that it may be clearly seen that his works have been carried out in God." – John 3:20-21

John's Gospel is represented by an eagle. Eagles symbolize heavenly things–things that come from above. John's Gospel focuses on how Jesus Himself came down from heaven to become human, die on the Cross, and rise again so that one day we could live eternally in His glory. After Jesus rose from the grave, He ascended back into Heaven. And even though Jesus' body isn't on earth anymore, He sent the Holy Spirit to guide and comfort us.

The Gospel of John is sort of the oddball out of the four Gospels. Instead of jumping into the story of Jesus' life, John starts out with a long, poetic description of who Jesus is and has been from the beginning of time: God Himself (Read John 1). John also uses a lot of symbolism in his witness- such as light and darkness. You can see in the verse above that two literal things are being used (light and darkness) to describe concepts that we can't always see (good and evil). Think of light and darkness as earthly concepts that can represent heavenly concepts.

Throughout John's Gospel, you can see that there are several instances of language that uses something physical (like bread or water) to represent something abstract (like spirit or life). John does this so that we, as readers, will be able to grasp the spiritual implications of Jesus' ministry here on Earth. He wanted to show us that there were big things happening in a spiritual sense and that Jesus' life has heavenly implications!

QUESTIONS

1. How does Jesus' life, death, and resurrection change your life right now, on this earth?

2. Even though John is written a little differently than the other three Gospels, why is it still a very valuable witness to Jesus' life, death, and resurrection?

3. Remember that we are all in need of God's love and Jesus' sacrifice for our salvation. How does the fact that Jesus came to earth for the sake of all sinners change the way you view other people (even the ones that you aren't so crazy about)?

DAY 19 — *JESUS, THE REAL ORIGIN STORY*

"In the beginning was the Word, and the Word was with God, and the Word was God. He was with God in the beginning. Through him all things were made; without him nothing was made that has been made. In him was life, and that life was the light of all mankind. The light shines in the darkness, and the darkness has not overcome it." -John 1:1-5

Any good character in a book or movie has a good origin story. An origin story is a backstory about how the character began and helps you understand who the character is and their motivations. Most of us think of Christmas, the birth of Jesus, as His origin story. But Jesus' real origin is that He has no 'origin' at all. He existed before the creation of all things! Read John 1:1-5. (Note: if you haven't studied these verses before, you may want to read them a few times as they are a little tough to follow at first).

Jesus' origin story doesn't start with a manager, it starts even before the very beginning of all things. Before Jesus came down to mankind as a baby, He existed in time and space with God the Creator. John is known for focusing on Jesus' divinity, and it certainly shines through in this origin story. The truth of these verses is super complex. Jesus has always been, because Jesus is God. Let that sink in for a minute... Though Jesus is God's Son, Jesus is also fully God Himself. It's a truth full of profound implications and mysteries! You might even spend the rest of your life thinking it over!

⚘ *Tip*

Here is one way to help you start understanding this big concept: Your parents and grandparents were obviously born before you. But take some time to really think about what their life was like before you were born. You might even ask them to tell you stories from when they were your age!

QUESTIONS

1. According to these verses, what do we know of Jesus' origin story before He arrived as a baby in a manger?

2. Look closely at the last half of today's passage. In your own words, what does it mean for Jesus to be the light that cannot be overcome by darkness?

3. How does this 'origin' story grow your faith in God?

DAY 20 — BURIAL

"Now in the place where he was crucified there was a garden, and in the garden a new tomb in which no one had yet been laid." – John 19:41

In John chapter 19, we see a wealthy man named Joseph of Arimathea who makes a special request to take and bury the body of Jesus. The government officials allowed him, and then various followers of Jesus took His body and laid it in a new tomb. They wrapped Him in all the wrappings that were customary for their people. It was a proper and respectful burial for what outsiders would have called a criminal.

While those burying Jesus mourned the loss of their friend, it must have felt like all hope was lost. Imagine thinking that the Light of the World had just been snuffed out like a candle. To make matters worse, many of Jesus' followers were completely blindsided by His death. They did not realize that this person they came to love and worship would suffer so much and ultimately die! But in their grief, they played a big role in God's plan to fulfill His promises.

Take a look at Isaiah 53:9.

> *And they made his grave with the wicked*
> *and with a rich man in his death,*
> *although he had done no violence,*
> *and there was no deceit in his mouth.*

Sound familiar? (If you need to, read John 19 again). Even in the midst of a burial, we see God's promises being fulfilled in Jesus Christ. Although His followers were possibly just trying to do the right and godly thing, they ended up becoming a piece of a beautiful and perfect story.

Can you think of a time when you felt like you had no hope? That's what Christ's followers felt. Even in the midst of a dark day, this truth remains: As long as God keeps His word, there is always a reason to hope! It's this hope that we can carry out into the world, professing that no matter how dark the world seems, the Light of the World in Christ always shines bright!

QUESTIONS

1. What are some ways you see God keeping His promises to His people, even today?

2. Why can you have hope, no matter how dark the world gets?

3. How can you share your hope in Christ with the world?

DAY 21 — *Easter Day* —

"Blessed be the God and Father of our Lord Jesus Christ! According to his great mercy, he has caused us to be born again to a living hope through the resurrection of Jesus Christ from the dead, to an inheritance that is imperishable, undefiled, and unfading, kept in heaven for you" -1 Peter 1:3-4

Today is a very special day... assuming you are reading this on Easter Sunday of course! Many people would say that when Christians gather to celebrate the resurrection of Christ, we celebrate the most important moment in our faith. In the verse above, Peter points to the resurrection of Jesus as the foundation for our hope, and the reason that we are also able to one day receive eternal life. And not just any kind of eternal life- one that is imperishable, undefiled, and unfading. What we receive in Jesus Christ is more than just a forgiveness of sins and a rescue from death. The death that your sins have earned is replaced with a life that is everlasting, meaningful, and full of joy in the Lord!

On Easter, we celebrate the resurrection of Jesus, and also that one day, we will experience eternal life after death. This is incredible news for believers and something that is certainly worth sharing with the world. Just like Matthew, Mark, Luke, and John, all believers will be witnesses to the Lord working in their lives. No, you won't have a first-hand account of what Jesus said on a mountain somewhere, but you will have a story to share. It starts with who you were before knowing Jesus, and how you've changed since. It can include how you've seen Him work in the lives of others- like how He has healed someone or intervened in a tough situation to give hope.

This Easter, take time to think about how you would share your witness. If you ever need help knowing how to tell others about who Jesus is, you have four incredible resources in the Gospels! Look at how these fellow believers took the time to point out different stories and characteristics of Jesus. And yet all of them still point to the death and resurrection of Jesus, and tell us about the impact that has on all who proclaim the name of the Lord. Due to the work of Jesus Christ on the Cross, you have a heavenly inheritance that cannot be taken away from you. The question now is, how is this going to change the way you live your life from here on out?

QUESTION

Today, there is just one question. That means, there is a lot of room for you to write down your answer! So here it goes: **How would you share your witness with others?**

HOW TO KNOW JESUS

Maybe you've turned to this page having never entered into a saving relationship with Jesus. Maybe you already have a saving relationship with Jesus and need to be more committed to making Him known. No matter where you find yourself, this page is for you. If you need to know Jesus, this page is an excellent place to start. If you need to make Jesus known, this page can help you think about how to go about sharing His story with others.

TO ENTER INTO A SAVING RELATIONSHIP WITH JESUS, YOU FIRST HAVE TO UNDERSTAND WHO GOD IS.

First, God is the Creator (Gen 1:1). He created everything, even you. Second, God is perfect in all His ways (Ps. 18:30). So, combined, that makes God the perfect creator of all things. He rules over everything, and His rule is 100% right.

NEXT, YOU HAVE TO ACCEPT THAT YOUR SIN IS A PROBLEM (ONE THAT YOU CAN'T SOLVE ON YOUR OWN).

Because God is the perfect King, when we do something that goes against His ways, it's called sin. And because God is who He is, all sin is rebellion against Him (Ps. 51:3-4). The only right penalty for our rebellion? It's death (Rom. 6:23). Both spiritual and physical. The worst part is that we're completely unable to save ourselves.

THEN, YOU HAVE TO GRASP THE TRUTH THAT JESUS IS THE ONLY ANSWER TO YOUR SIN PROBLEM.

Jesus is God's on, sent to earth to live a perfect life so that He might serve as the once-and-for-all perfect sacrifice in our place (Matt. 1:18-21). Jesus died on the cross to satisfy God's sense of justice and save from their sins all who will believe in Him (Jon 3:16). Only Jesus could do this.

FINALLY, YOU HAVE TO BELIEVE IN YOUR HEART THAT JESUS IS WHO HE SAYS HE IS AND THAT HIS DEATH ACCOMPLISHED WHAT HE SAID IT ACCOMPLISHED.

The only way to be saved from sin is to believe that Jesus is who He says He is. When we put our faith in Jesus as our Savior, we're saved from the penalty of our sin. We're saved from death. This is only possible by God's grace through faith in Jesus. We can't do anything to earn our salvation. Here's the coolest part: When you come to salvation in Christ, your life is completely renewed, freed from the effects of sin (2 Cor. 5:17). You are a new creation!

IF YOU NEED TO COME TO FAITH IN JESUS, LET THESE WORDS GUIDE YOU. AND IF YOU KNOW SOMEONE THAT NEEDS CHRIST, USE THIS TO HELP YOU SHARE THE GOSPEL WITH THEM.

THANK YOU TO OUR AUTHORS

Thomas Gray

Jon LaMarque

Sarah Beth Richardson

Anna Russell

Amber Warren

A 3-PART DEVOTIONAL EXPERIENCE
DESIGNED TO HELP YOU BECOME A DISCIPLE OF CHRIST.

NEW: FIRST STEPS FOR NEW CHRIST-FOLLOWERS	NEXT: GROWING A FAITH THAT LASTS	NOW: IMPACTING YOUR WORLD FOR CHRIST (RIGHT NOW!)
A powerful 4-week experience to help you get off to a strong start on our journey with Jesus. Build a firm foundation by understanding what changes when you are alive with Jesus.	4-weeks to guide you in taking ownership of your faith. What is life's purpose and what it has to do with God's mission. Learn to implement spiritual habits to transform you life.	Do not wait until later to make an impact for Jesus, you can do it NOW! This 4-week experience will open your eyes to the everyday opportunities you have to live for Jesus NOW!, not just in the future.

WITNESS
21-DAY EASTER DEVOTIONAL

PUBLISHED BY YM360

TABLE OF
contents

Director of Publishing: Kerry Ray
General Editor: Amber Warren
Graphic Design: Morgan Williams